Frontispiece: Edith and Ron Pinhorn with their grandfather Fred Ford in around 1896, standing under a tree on what was to become the site of the Congregational chapel, Hilbury Road, Alderholt.

Pat Buckingham   2000

IMAGES
of England

AROUND
VERWOOD

Compiled by
Jo Draper and Penny Copland Griffiths

TEMPUS

First published 1999
Copyright © Jo Draper and Penny Copland Griffiths, 1999

Tempus Publishing Limited
The Mill, Brimscombe Port,
Stroud, Gloucestershire, GL5 2QG

ISBN 0 7524 1538 7

Typesetting and origination by
Tempus Publishing Limited
Printed in Great Britain by
Midway Clark Printing, Wiltshire

This book is dedicated to the kind people of Verwood, Alderholt, Crendell, Cripplestyle, Horton, Holt and Wimborne St Giles, who have lent us so many wonderful photographs.

Ted Saunders of Ebblake, Verwood, with his bus, which travelled the area in the 1930s. It visited Salisbury three times a week for the market, taking an hour for the short journey. Chickens and small animals were welcome on the bus.

Home Farm (left) and Manor Farm Alderholt, probably in the 1920s. The pond and the old brick farmhouses look like a picture-book illustration. The Scammels farmed at Manor Farm and the Nicklens at Home Farm. In the 1920s Mrs Mary Scammel was running Manor Farm: she was one of three women farmers listed at Alderholt. Both houses survive beside the road to Alderholt Mill, but the pond has gone. Its restoration has been suggested as a Millennium project.

Contents

Watching the world go by at Crendell in 1961 – Harry Lane (left) Edgar Lockyer and George Manston under the finger-post. The first two were hurdle-makers, part of the important woodland industries of the area.

By the Dorset Farmers lorry in 1929 are, from left to right: Frederick Prior, Harry Adlam (from Sixpenny Handley), Mr Sherry, Tom Haskell (from Woodlands). Dorset Farmers was a co-operative firm established to supply farmers cheaply and efficiently and to sell corn. The Verwood branch (which had its stores at the station) was established in the early 1920s.

Introduction

Verwood has always been on the edge of many things: right on the boundary between the counties of Dorset and Hampshire; on the edge of the New Forest (but not part of it); and only just into agriculture because the land was so poor.

The name Verwood or Fairwood is known from 1329, and is recorded as early as 1288 as Beubos or Beau Bois – the same name but French. Until 1887 Verwood didn't even exist as a parish – Alderholt and Verwood were part of the huge parish of Cranborne. This was true of other adjoining areas: Holt was part of Wimborne, West Moors was part of West Parley and Woodlands was in Horton parish. The old villages (and their parishes) are easily identified because they have old churches: Hampreston and West Parley down on the River Stour; Holt, Horton, Wimborne St Giles, Edmonsham and Cranborne straddling the heathland and the clays and chalk. The long swathe of heathlands running north-south through West Moors, Verwood and Alderholt does not have a single ancient parish. The original Cranborne parish contained 13,000 acres, much of it moor and heathland, and Wimborne (which included Holt) was nearly 12,000 acres. By contrast the adjacent parish of Hinton Parva was less than 500 acres, but on fertile land.

Although divided from the New Forest by the big valley of the River Avon (the county boundary), the Verwood area is really very similar to the New Forest. In both cases the geology (clays, gravels and sands) has produced poor agricultural land. Verwood and Alderholt were part of Cranborne Chase, a medieval hunting enclosure like the New Forest itself. Poor land was often used for hunting as it was less valuable.

The occupations of the people of Verwood in the 1898 *Directory* show what an unusual village it was even at the end of the nineteenth century. Verwood had two bakers, two public houses, three shops, a bootmaker, two grocers, three blacksmiths, a bricklayer, two coal merchants, a horse dealer and two carpenters and wheelwrights. These trades would be found in every large village, along with Verwood's eleven farmers, one market gardener, a threshing machine hirer and three cow-keepers. What is odd are the sixteen broom-makers, four brickmakers, six potters and six earthenware dealers. These represent the specific woodland and marginal land occupations, and the three hawkers and eight higglers (all travelling salesmen) must have depended on the potters and broom-makers for their goods to sell. Clearly Verwood was very different.

The 1867 Agricultural Commission found that on the heathland, reclamation often consisted of letting 'a large piece of land to a labourer on a lease for lives, with permission to build upon it. The result has been the erection of a large number of miserable cottages, occupied by these life owners, and never repaired. (Verwood's cottages are described later in the report as 'very bad'). The population exceeds the wants of the district, and a large number of the men work on the farms only in the summer, and go to the woods or do any sort of work that they can get for a living in the winter'.

William Chafin noted the dependence on woodland and coppicing in the late-eighteenth century. He drew a sentimental and condescending picture of 'the industrious peasant who hath acquired a small pittance, sufficient to enable him to purchase a few spar gads for employment in the long winter evenings … and while the master of the cottage is attentive to his work, and his good dame busy in her household concerns, the children are employed in picking up the chips and shreds of the gads, and with handfuls at a time feed the lingering fire underneath the little crock, containing a few potatoes or other vegetables, the produce of their small garden plot … and the little blaze from each handful adds a temporary lustre to the dimness of their farthing candle' (he was making spars from hazel for thatching).

The Verwood area was always attractive to those trying to set up in farming because the land was cheap, but the poor land often defeated the settlers. Ralph Wightman recalled the area between the wars, when virtually every landholder was 'a stranger who was tempted by the relative cheapness of the land and the nearness of Bournemouth into thinking that he could grow market-garden crops. Most of the little holdings have a sad history of continual change of occupants'. This had been true of Verwood and the surrounding area all through its history. Some few succeeded, particularly those who potted or made brooms as well as growing crops, but many failed.

Verwood is now a town and, in 1996, had 11,000 inhabitants, its own council and a mayor. The abrupt changes from heathland to farmland, or heathland to houses, still remain.

Acknowledgements

We are grateful to Tony Bradshaw for much information on all the farming photographs; to the Veteran Car Club of Great Britain for identifying the car on p.113; to Sheena Pearce for word-processing and to the Dorset County Library for much information. The local *Directories* (Kellys, P.O. etc.) have been used extensively, and *The Anecdotes and History of Cranborne Chase* (Second Edition) (1818) by William Chafin. Two articles are from the *Dorset Year Book* 'Stephen Pope, Cripplestyle' by S. Clement (1939, pp. 129-131) and 'Hand Made Brooms (John Haskell of Verwood)' (1938, p.98). Ralph Wightman *The Wessex Heathland* (1953); 'A survey of Moorlands near Verwood' by Heywood Sumner (*Proceedings of the Dorset Natural History and Archaeological Society* Vol.54 (1932) pp. 232-240; and the same author's *The New Forest* (1924) along with *General View of the Agriculture of the County of Dorset* (1815) by William Stevenson have much detail on the heathlands. *The Story of the Congregational Churches of Dorset* (1899) by W. Densham and J. Ogle has been very useful, as have two memoirs: *Grampy: Sidney Frampton of Holtwood* (1983) by Pam Bailey; and Cliff Lockyer's memories of life in the area. Alderholt's history is to be found in *Records of Alderholt* (Second Edition, 1997) by Lady Smith-Gordon, Fred and Donald Hibbert, and *A Century of Service: 1894-1994 Alderholt Parish Council* (1994) by Stanley Broomfield. *The Verwood and District Potteries* (1987) by David Algar, Anthony Light and Penny Copland Griffiths details the history of the potteries.

For the loan of photographs, we are extremely grateful to the following people for their contributions. (Numbers refer to pages and A and B to upper and lower illustrations respectively.) Dennis Bailey: 19B, 43A, 45, 47B, 48B, 54A, 55B, 56-58, 59B, 64. Maud Brewer:10A, 15, 16B, 18B, 21, 27, 35, 36B, 44, 49. Stanley Sims and Winifred Broomfield: the cover photograph, 14, 25, 32A. Judith Bond and Peter Lane: 46. Rita Bright p.32B, 34A, 61-63. Biddy Cannell: 31, 34B. Julian Comrie: 43A. Frank Cutler: 94A, 96, 97B, 98. Dorset County Museum, Dorchester: 10B. Ack Monkton Farm: 48A, 55A, 90-91, 101, 112, 118-124, 128A. Peter Gould: 47A, 88B. Joyce Harwood: 103, 105B. Chris King: 92. John Leach: 38A. Cliff Lockyer: 6A. George Orman: 20, 22A, 125, 127. Rosie Pitman and Kitty Cox: 6B, 11B, 22A, 23-24, 26B, 28A, 29B, 42B. Tom, Mike and Mary Seeviour: 105A, 114A. John Sherman: 5, 52, 68A, 70B, 75A, 76B, 81A. Geoff and Helen Tyler: 30A, 39, 41A, 89, 92A, 93, 95A, 97A, 107A, 114B, 115-116, 117A, 126A, 128B. Barrie Wallis: 2, 4, 13, 51, 82-87, 88A. Ian Waterfield: 30B. Dennis Wharton: 94B, 95B, 99, 104, 110B, 111, 113. Kevin Zebedee: 33A, 60A. Betty Zebedee: 59A, 60B. Any not listed are in the Authors' collections. Our thanks to all those people, too numerous to mention, who have supplied factual information and helped identify places and people.

One

Verwood

The inhabitants of marginal lands were more independent than those in richer parishes because most of the heathland men worked for themselves rather than a farmer or big landowner. In 1899 Three Legged Cross Verwood was described as having a scattered population 'and the district somewhat dreary and barren, but the people seem fairly prosperous, and have a good deal of independence, living as they do, mostly, at small rentals, on their own leasehold plots, which they or their fathers enclosed from the surrounding waste' (Congregational History).

Dewlands Common, the south-western part of Verwood, probably 1930s. Winding gravel lanes, scattered brick villas and cottages with occasional hedgerow trees, typical of the area because there were no real village centres until the later twentieth century. The heathland commons provided fuel as well as grazing. In 1870, a journalist from *Good Words* visited a cottage near Wimborne, possibly in Verwood, where turf was the usual fuel. They needed 3,000 turves a winter, and had to pay 2s 6d per thousand, and 12s carriage. This sounds very little, but the labourer only earned 9s a week.

Children playing (and even swimming) at Higher Moor Verwood, 1900-1910. The heath is what makes Verwood, Alderholt and the adjoining parishes different. The land was poor, so there was little agriculture, and many small industries developed.

Conifers at Alderholt, probably 1930s. There were a few older clumps and small woods at Alderholt before forestation began. These are probably one of the older plantings. From 1928 the Forestry Commission took over huge areas of the Verwood heathland, and 3,500 acres were being planted with conifers by 1932. A nursery was established at Plumley Farm and between forty and sixty men were employed each winter to plant the trees. The ancient bogs were drained before planting commenced, revealing at Wild Church Bottom the remains of many small trees preserved in the peat, indicating that at least parts of the area had once been woodland. Heywood Sumner described the plantings in 1932, and hoped 'that the Forestry Commissioners of AD 2,000 will be like-minded with those of 1928, who agreed to the preservation of fine groups of trees, of belts of trees and of landmark clumps' when they felled parts of their plantings in the New Forest.

A drawing by Heywood Sumner of the trees on Mount Ararat in 1932 (also seen below). The prominent hill on Boveridge Heath is named after the mountain on which Noah's ark came to rest after the flood. The name is only known from the nineteenth century. Four old pines marked the top of Mount Ararat, and water had washed away the soil from their roots, producing a strange effect. 'These unlovely pines clinging to their hill-top in spite of warring elements and wasting soil, express the grim genius of endurance that abides in moorland life' (Sumner in Verwood survey, 1932). The heathland had earlier kept the small population in turf for fuel and 'a few cattle are kept on various parts of the heaths, and some poor half-starved sheep are occasionally seen wandering about' (1815 *General View*).

Left: Rose Ferret with her children Rosie and Kitty (in hats) and a cousin from London picnicking at Mount Ararat in August 1928. *Right*: Rose Ferret's cousin George at the same spot.

11

Ruined cob cottages: a drawing (above) by Gerald Summers, 1922 and (below) the results of a fire, probably also 1920s. Both cottages were 'mud-built' which is cob, with brick chimneys. One was thatched, the other had a tile roof. Cob cottages were common in the area, but most of them have disappeared.

Single-storey thatched cob cottage at Alderholt, known as Mrs Upton's cottage, and long since demolished. It stood near the road to Fordingbridge. Many cob cottages survive in Three Legged Cross, and the potteries and other industries used sheds built of cob.

Heywood Sumner described the proper building of a cob or mud wall in *The New Forest* (1924): the material should be 'sandy, clayey loam with small stones in it: and with heath [heather], rushes, and sedge-grass, or straw, thoroughly puddled into the mass by trampling. In the best-made mud walls this was dobbed and bonded by the mud-waller with his trident mud-prong in successive layers. About two feet, vertical, being raised at a time, then left for ten days to dry' before the next layer was added. 'Walls built thus, on heathstone or brick footings, stand well'. He complained of poor mud walls 'raised without any footings, and by inexperienced "mudders" who used the wrong sort of clay; who did not temper it still with heath; and who could not build a wall with a mud-prong, but trusted to board "clamps" and thus this serviceable walling material has been discredited, most unfairly'. He added that for 'excellent mud-walling' he would 'go to Verwood; to Mr Sims of Sutton Holmes, Verwood, who has inherited the knowledge of his craft, and can point out this, that, and the other mud-walled, thatched cottage in his native village, as built by his grandfather, his father, or himself'.

Sidney Frampton of Holtwood recalled the methods used in the 1930s. Concrete was then preferred for foundations, whereas stone had earlier been used. First a cartload of clay was needed. 'Then you use water to make the clay wet and then tread the mixture well, then turn it over with a prong and tread it again. When you've done that a time or two you put green heather into it. Then you turn it again and keep on treading it and adding more heather until the texture is right – until it is stiff enough to stay on the prong. You start by plumping it down on the wall, eighteen inches wide, building it up to eighteen inches high. You must do this in one day'. After about four days another layer can be added.

Edith Barrow (later Sims), Ellen Sims with her son and Annie Sims (from left to right) outside a new house in Ringwood Road, Verwood, called 'Millford', in around 1895-1900. The bicycle perhaps belonged to the photographer. At first glance this house looks like the usual villa of around 1900, but closer examination shows that the walls are of cob, not even rendered to disguise the lines left by the different levels left as it was built. It has not been converted from an old cottage because the proportions are wrong, and there are no indications of heightening or old windows. The roof is made from corrugated iron, and the chimneys of brick. The villa is an extraordinary combination of an age-old method of building (cob) with 'modern' style (proper 'villa' not a cottage) and material (corrugated iron).

The painted house (right) is probably also built of cob, and was in Ringwood Road. In the 1920s, Heywood Sumner was an enthusiast for cob walls. If built well they 'stand firm and impervious for generations, and provide warmth in winter and coolness in summer within the cottages, and they cost less than walls of any other material'. In modern terms, they provide very good insulation, and if, as in the old saying, supplied with a good hat and a good pair of shoes (a good footing and roof) they are just as long-lived as other walls.

A rural view of Ringwood Road, c. 1900, with children posed to improve the view.

Cross Roads was a quiet part of Verwood, with the Congregational chapel and a pottery there since about 1800 and very few houses until after 1900. Now it is the town centre. Top Cross Roads Pottery is shown here in 1942; still potting despite the Second World War. This workshop is built of cob, with footings of brick. Traditional bread pans are lined up on boards in the yard awaiting firing. It must have been impossible to black-out the kilns when they were being fired.

The Congregational chapels at Cross Roads were next to the pottery. The further one was built in 1877, and was also used as a school, which became full-time after the second chapel was built in 1906. It continued as a school until 1967, and is now the library. The triangular open space (now a car park) had been used as a clay pit.

Two later views of Cross Roads, probably 1930s, after many more houses had been built. Nellie Hopkins had a newsagents and stationers at Cross Roads from the late 1920s and it is still run by the Hopkins family. Mabel Whitemore's ironmongery was there from around the same date into the later 1930s.

The Manor Road, Verwood.

Manor Road, *c.* 1906, leading towards Three Legged Cross, with many new houses. Verwood had a small brick industry from the eighteenth century, but after the railway arrived in the 1870s, many more cottages and villas were built, most of them of brick. The new Congregational chapel (background right) still has scaffolding around it. It opened in 1906.

Ye Resting House, Verwood.

Ye Restinge House, Ringwood Road, was a village reading room and library which cost 2d weekly for the Reading Room and 1d each for library books. A billiard room was also provided, along with lunches and teas. Reading rooms were usually for locals only, but at Verwood the Restinge House advertised accommodation for cyclists and apartments with or without food. In effect it was a pub without the alcohol: in 1911 it was advertising itself as Coffee Rooms. It seems to have closed in the later 1930s, and became a shop.

Vicarage Road, Verwood, probably 1920s. Ralph Wightman remembered Verwood in the 1920s and 1930s, when 'every road through this part of the heath was lined with small houses or bungalows' and many of the houses were 'set back from the roads amongst tall coniferous trees. Rhododendrons, azaleas and lupins grow freely on this acid soil … to a farmer's eye the prospect is poor, but an artist can turn his back on little red-brick houses and always find a pine tree against the sky or a silver birch beside a pool'.

Job Brewer of Verwood, wearing his traditional smock. The photograph is difficult to date precisely, but is late nineteenth century, when smock-wearing was becoming uncommon. He holds a whip, the usual symbol of a carter, the farm labourer who looked after horses on the farm. He and the horses did the ploughing and any other work needing their motive power. The crude shed behind is thatched with heather, and has a pile of brushwood (right): it may have been a broom-maker's workshop.

The members of Women's Social Hour photographed in the garden of Mrs Cannell's house in Verwood, June 1928, soon after it was formed. The highlight of the garden party was the group photograph. The Women's Social Hour motto was 'Helping One Another'. Mrs Grout was the President. From left to right, back row (standing): Mrs Cannell Snr, Mrs Chiverton, Mrs Reeks, Mrs Agnes Thorne, Mrs Lush, Mrs Kitty Palmer, Mrs Price, Mrs Savage, Mrs Oxford, Jane Haskell, Mrs Toms, -?-, Mrs Orman, -?-, Mrs Chambers. Front Row: -?-, Mrs Grout (President for thirty years), Mrs Morgan, Mrs Seaton, Mrs Hopkins, Mrs Fred Brewer, Mrs Sims, Mrs Tom Sims, Mrs Flemington, Mrs Gilbert, Mrs Varder.

The Women's Social Hour in the later 1930s, this time in summer dresses. In the back row: second from left is Mrs Chiverton, fourth from left Mrs Chambers, sixth from left Mrs Grout (President). Second row from back: far right Mrs Giles Sims. Third row (seated): second from left Miss Varder, fourth from left Mrs Thorpe, third from right Mrs Hopkins, fourth from right Mrs Seaton, fifth from right Mrs Gilbert. The women were from the Methodist and Congregational churches, and met once a fortnight for talks, singing etc. Even the small children wear hats.

Swimming at Does Hatch on the River Crane, Verwood 1920s. Only boys swam or paddled in the very muddy-looking and probably very cold water. The only person identified is Ralph Haskell (above: arms folded, below: arms akimbo).

The Orman family outside their house in Lake Road, Verwood, in the 1930s. The house probably dates from the 1920s.

Mr and Mrs Prior at their gate at Burnbrook House, Moneyfly, Verwood. The house looks like a child's drawing, with its five neat windows and central door. It was probably built around 1900. The Priors moved to Verwood in 1911/12, and were poultry and general farmers. Poultry farming expanded greatly between 1910 and 1920, and was particularly common in Verwood and surrounding area because the heathlands were cheap land.

Rosie (left) and Kitty Prior, aged five and three years old. They were the granddaughters of Mr and Mrs Prior (opposite). The photograph was taken at school. Kitty, who was not old enough to be at school, went along especially to be in the photograph.

Rosie and Kitty, at an older age and both just returned from school, showing off their new brother, Fred, in the pram.

Rosie Prior with her father Fred in 1929. Motorbikes first started to become common in the 1920s, although they were still relatively expensive. This machine was six years old in 1929 – it was first registered (to another owner) in 1923. Fred worked for the Verwood branch of the Dorset Farmers (see p. 8).

Rose Prior, Rosie and Kitty's mother, in 1929, with poultry.

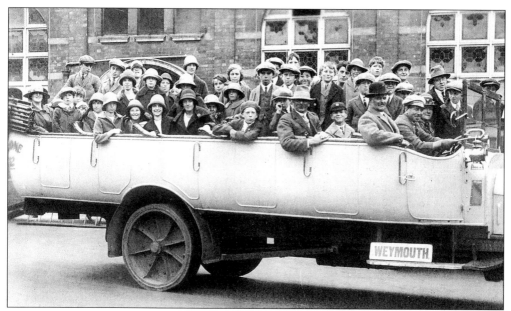

Verwood Methodist Sunday School outing to Weymouth in 1926. The charabanc came from Broads of Fordingbridge. Between the Wars, when cars were rare, outings like these were greatly appreciated. Cliff Lockyer remembers similar trips from Alderholt either to Weymouth or Bournemouth. 'You can imagine the excitement and cheers when we all saw the sea'. The trip took two hours each way and they would 'arrive home about 8p.m., tired and perhaps irritable after a long day out'.

Verwood Football Club, 1920-21. From left to right, back row: Ted Sandy (linesman), J. Brewer (President), ? Willis (referee), Captain Morris Ferrett, ? Manuel, Norman Barratt, K. Burrow (secretary), Aubrey Burrow (with collecting box). Middle row: Fred Shearing, J. Bailey (vice-captain), K. Brewer (assistant secretary). Front row: J. Davies, J. Shearing, W. Shearing, G. Brewer, Revd Rider.

The school at Verwood, probably 1920s. It was founded in the 1840s and makes a fine group with the church (right). The school is now St Michael's Centre and has been extended, but the school house still looks just the same as the postcard.

Verwood school in 1931. From left to right, back row: Jim Churchill, Wilfred Sims, Robert Cool, -?-, Jim Crocker, Roy Price, Geoffrey Gilbert(?), Tom Barrow. Middle row: -?-, Kathleen Sims, Rosemary Thorne, Jessie Ferrett, Rosie Prior, Edna Shearing, Lily Bumstead, -?-. Front Row: Howard Cox, Geoffrey Lockyer(?), Monsell Shearing, Alec Shearing.

Verwood school in 1917 (above) and *c.* 1915 (below). Verwood Undenominational school opened in 1907. It had to attract students, so in November 1907 'a Public tea and lantern lecture' was given 'to gather intending pupils together'. Views of London and Dorset were shown. Twenty full-time and four half-time pupils were immediately enrolled. In these First World War period photographs, all the boys have wide 'eton' collars, and almost all the girls wear white overalls which must have been really difficult to keep clean. The photograph (below) includes: back row fifth from left Len Sims, middle row extreme right Clifford Sims, front row left Agnes Reeks, front row second from right Gwen Brewer.

Verwood Station, 1920s. The man in a white shirt in the middle is Fred Prior. The construction of the railway in the 1870s helped local industries because goods could be transported more easily. A large brick manufactory was established right by the station. From 1915 it was called the Verwood and Gotham Brick and Tile Company, and was served by its own goods siding until 1945. The railway closed in 1964. Milk was transported by rail – churns are parked on the right. The Albion Hotel (centre) was actually in the station yard.

Looking across the drying sheds of the Verwood and Gotham Brick and Tile Company's works, probably around 1910.

Station Road, Verwood, probably 1920s. The railway ran to the west of the village, and encouraged building to spread that way.

The new porter at Verwood Station, probably 1930s. The name is not known, but he does look smart.

Romford Bridge, around 1900-1910. Romford is on the River Crane, and although it seems part of Verwood, technically it is in Edmondsham parish. Romford was a small separate hamlet, and may have medieval origins. The cart road down into the river was for fetching water, and also to drive carts into the river in the summer to swell their dried-out wooden wheels.

Romford Farm, around 1900-1910.

The 1931 cookery class at Verwood. From left to right, back row: Betty Biggin, -?-, Joyce Harman. Front row: Betty Gilhooly, Peggy Northeast, -?-, Nora Hugett.

Mrs Biddy Cannell (née Karslake) with her motorbike in June 1931. She taught the girls from the Verwood Council school every Tuesday and Friday in an old hut shared at other times with the boy's woodwork class, where the present Police Station now stands. She had up to twelve girls aged 11-14 in her class. As there was no running water, a Mr Sims drew it early in the morning from the local stream before the class commenced. The girls learnt how to deal with everyday cooking, with vegetables in season and at appropriate times making Marmalade, jams and Christmas cake. Many a Verwood woman owes her cooking skills to Mrs Cannell's careful teaching. Mrs Cannell arrived on her two-stroke Excelsior motor bike, dressed in her ordinary clothes with a thick home-made jersey (made by herself), a pair of jodhpurs (a gift), golf socks, leather jacket, gauntlet gloves and leather helmet (which had been given by a friend who was in the Royal Flying Corps in the First World War I). She braved the elements to teach not only girls from Verwood, but also travelling to the schools at Wimborne St Giles (Mondays and Thursdays) and Moor Critchel (Wednesdays). Her husband became one of the youngest Chairmen of the Parish Council during the war years.

Mr John Barrow, baker and grocer of Verwood, around 1900-1910. His trap is smartly painted, and he seems to be carrying sacks of grain.

Members of the Zebedee, Fry and Roberts families at Verwood Carnival, later 1940s. Horses were still shown then. Verwood Carnival started in a small way in 1929, and grew enormously in the 1930s.

Art Zebedee (left) and Amanda Harris at the Verwood Carnival, 1960s. Art does not seem to have mastered handbag and skirt very well.

Verwood Carnival, 1950s. 'A woman's work is never done'.

Verwood Brownies in 1935 at Verwood Carnival, not really looking very threatening as pirates.

Two

The Potteries

In East Dorset the earliest records show that potting was taking place in 1260. Verwood became the most important centre in the late history of the industry, and the last pottery, known as Cross Roads, only closed in 1952. With an abundance of clay locally, pottery-making became a way of life for villagers in the surrounding area, supporting many men, women and children in the various jobs that were required to produce the earthenware pottery. An abundance of documentary and photographic evidence survives on this important industry showing how it enabled these villages to survive. Over forty sites are known and as the area expands and housing increases more sites may come to light.

Potters at Verwood Carnival, c. 1928. Mrs Biddy Cannell, who was on the Carnival Committee, recalls that one year the potters erected a tent, brought down their wheel and, for 1s, allowed the public to try and throw a pot. She remembers trying to make a pot herself with little success, but she enjoyed the experience as did many other people. Here we have the potters with their display on a wagon.

From a unique film of 1917 made by Charles Urban, this image shows the method of pottery manufacture at the last working pottery, Cross Roads. Here the boys are preparing the clay by treading it by foot to make it the right consistency for throwing pots. The film was discovered in an old cinema in Derbyshire and donated to the Potteries Trust by Lesley Heywood, Honorary Curator of Poole Pottery Museum. In the middle is Len Sims who worked at the pottery from when he left school in 1917 until closure in 1952.

A newspaper cutting of Len Sims dated 3 May 1950, showing the method of treading clay which continued up to when the pottery closed in 1952.

A still from the same 1917 film. A worker, possibly Mr Ferret, on the left is wedging the clay for the potter Fred Fry, on the right, to make pots. Fred Fry the potter, preacher and Sunday school teacher, is remembered for the set of musical flower pots which he made and played. He ran the business from around just after the turn of the century until 1925 when he sold the pottery to Mr Robert Thorne. The boy sitting in the foreground is waiting to turn the wheel for the potter to throw pots.

A still from the 1917 film showing Fred Fry putting a handle on a jug (known as a pitcher). This low slung, bellied pot is typical of the simple vessels produced at Verwood. Note the posy basket in the background.

A newspaper cutting from Bernard Leach's private papers in the Holborne Museum, Bath, showing Fred Fry throwing pots. The caption reads 'Where time halts. No modern inventions are used by this potter on the eastern borders of Dorset; he plies his trade in the same crude way as his ancestors have done for 200 years'. The cutting is probably from the 1920s. When Bernard Leach returned from his travels in Japan, and before he continued his work in St Ives, he turned to the country potteries to revive the traditional way of making pots. Len Sims recalled a famous potter from Cornwall visiting the pottery. It is likely that this was Bernard Leach.

Extract from the 1917 film showing Fred Sims and possibly Bert Bailey carrying out flower pots on boards to dry outside.

A very early postcard, possibly 1905, showing the pottery drying outside. After throwing, this was the next procedure in the manufacture of earthenware. In the summer, pots were dried outside on boards and in the winter inside by means of heath and turf fires. Blackened roof timbers bear witness to this inside drying process in the one remaining shed at this site.

Another very early postcard. Handwritten on the front is 'General view of pottery Verwood'. In the background one can see the hills, a far cry from the view one would see now from the old Cross Roads Pottery. The buildings are the same as the other photograph (above), both built of cob, but one thatched, one tiled.

This photograph, probably dating from the early 1920s, shows the workers, most likely Len Sims on the left and George (known as 'Drummer') Brewer on the right, glazing pots. An extract from T.W. Wake Smart's personal notes in his *A Chronicle of Cranborne and the Cranborne Chase* (1841), gives the method of glazing as of remote date and as follows:- 'After the ware is formed it is set aside to dry and in about 24 hours is sufficiently firm to take the glaze. The glaze is made by melting metallic lead until reduced to a black powder, (or) as an oxide which is mixed with barley meal for use. $2\frac{1}{2}$ cwt of lead is mixed with two bushels of meal. The surface of the vessel is then moistened by a small mop dipped in a mixture of cow dung and water and the glaze being dusted over, it adheres to it. They are now ready for the kiln. This method was practised from early times until the dangers of lead began to be known. Parliament passed an Act banning the use of pure lead and the potters changed their method by obtaining a more safe substance called galena, which was obtained from Liverpool in powder form, mixed with water and applied by brush'. It is this later method that the workers are using in the photograph.

A still from the 1917 film showing the workers with Fred Fry (in the black waistcoat and bringing up the rear) taking the wood to the kiln to commence the firing.

Another old postcard with handwritten description 'Entrance to kiln Verwood Pottery'. No one yet has recognized this shed.

Fred Fry looking out of the chamber of the kiln, a still taken from the 1917 film. Note the large bushel pans on the right.

Fred Fry stoking the kiln, from the 1917 film. He is feeding the flue with brushwood – probably local hazel. The flames run into the kiln and lick around the pottery which is being fired. It took three days and two nights to fire a kiln.

A display by Fred Fry at a garden fête in Cranborne in 1909. Many of the pots shown here are not typical of the vessels generally produced at Verwood. They may relate to his friendship with the renowned archaeologist and landowner General Pitt-Rivers, who commissioned him to reproduce pots from his collection (some from overseas) in order to give to his friends as presents.

A Costrel or Dorset owl, a famous shape produced in these potteries and now perhaps the most generally recognised Dorset vessel. This one could have been made in the potteries in Alderholt. The incised inscription reads 'Samuel Read Alderholt Dorset August 30th 1869'. Samuel's granddaughter recalls that her father recounted this as being presented to his grandfather on his first day working at the potteries. The costrels were used by farm labourers to take beer or cider into the fields when they were working.

Frederick 'Pans' Brewer, a devoted officer in the Methodist church and Sunday school teacher, is remembered for selling pottery by wagon. Many relatives of the potters supported the industry in this fashion, travelling to the Isle of Wight, Portland, Trowbridge, Southampton, Farnham, Beaminster and Lyme Regis, in order to sell their wares. There are records of several Hawkers and this continued well into the latter days of the industry.

After Fred Fry sold the business in 1925, Mr Robert Thorne purchased the pottery and installed Mesheck Sims as potter. The pottery continued under his control and then under potter Bert Bailey (who had worked under both Fred Fry and Mesheck for many years) until it finally closed in 1952. From left to right: Len Sims, Mesheck Sims, Bert Bailey, Jim Scammell. (The date written on the reverse of this card is 4 August 1929).

Three
Besoms, Hurdles and Spars

The Verwood area was important for hurdle, spar, and broom-making as well as pottery and bricks. It was particularly well-placed for hurdles: the coppice woodlands for hazel grew well on the nearby clays, and the chalk downlands beyond had thousands of sheep needing hurdling. It is said that there were still fifteen hurdle-makers around Cranborne in 1955, and earlier there were many more. Besom brooms were a local speciality, using local heather or birch.

Wilf Foster of Crendell making thatching spars. Hurdle-makers also produced these long split hazel rods (stacked in the background) needed to peg thatch on a roof or a rick. When thatch was more common and every farm had ricks which needed thatching, hundreds of thousands of spars were needed every year.

Len Lane making a hurdle in the winter of 1936/7. At this time hurdles cost 6d (2½p) each, and were still used in their thousands for penning sheep. The hurdle he is working on has a gap known as a twilly hole to make them easier to carry: when hurdles were used for penning sheep they were moved frequently. Recent hurdles don't need a hole, and don't usually have it. The main tool for hurdling is the bill-hook, seen here parked on a stump. The hurdle-makers' boast is that he can make one faster than anyone else can pull one to pieces.

Peter Gould and James Moore laid this hedge in the traditional way along one of Peter's fields in Alderholt, 1990s. Cliff Lockyer remembers the hazel coppices being cut for the hurdle and spar makers and laid down in long lines (called drifts) approximately seven or eight yards apart. They must have looked just like this.

Len Lane showing local children how to make hurdles, probably in the 1970s. Walter Leonard Lane (always known as Len) was born in 1906 and died in 1988. He travelled around the area to find suitable coppices and, while working, discovered Rockborne Roman villa. Adders love coppices, and Len could kill them with one shot of his catapult.

Sheep at South Monkton Farm, in traditional hurdle enclosures (with a little straw roof) and feeding from a crib also made from hazel (and probably made by a local hurdle-maker). The shepherd holds his crook, and in the background (right) is the shepherd's hut. The sheep are probably soon to lamb. The photograph dates from 1941. The hurdle-makers were only part of the woodland industries. Cliff Lockyer remembers the many timber-cutters in the 1930s. Some, called strappers, cut the woods, laid hedges, and tied up faggots of brushwood for bedding hay and corn rick, and bavins which were similar but made of even lighter wood for burning in ovens.

The Cripplestyle Congregational chapel band, known as the Spar and Hurdle Band because so many of its members were hurdle-makers. They played for the annual Whitsun celebration at the chapel (see p. 56). From left to right, back row: -?-, John Sims, Arthur Bailey, Percy Nicklen, George Colbourne, Alf Lockyer, -?-. Front row, the boys are Wilf Foster (left) and Fred Sims (extreme right). Earlier nuts had also been important. William Chafin described the annual nutting in the woods of Cranborne Chase in the eighteenth century. People from all the hamlets and villages for miles around moved to the woods 'and make their abode there for whole weeks at a time'. After the days nutting ' they make large fires, which they sit around, eat their scanty meal, then slip from the green shells their day's gathering, talk over their success, [and] crack their jokes as well as their nuts'.

John Haskell, besom broom-maker of Verwood. Three Legged Cross was the centre of the industry, with fourteen broom-makers listed in the 1898 Directory (there were only twenty-four in the whole county). They declined to four in 1923, and by 1939 there was only one listed.

John Haskell (right) with Reg Hayward, probably 1920s. In 1938, John Haskell recalled that brooms had originally been made of heather, and were greatly in demand for sweeping out stables, but by the 1930s, the brooms were of birch and mostly used in gardens. He also made the handles of birch, stripping off the bark before forcing it into a bundle of birch. 'Sleets' (thin shavings of hazel) had been used to tie the bundles to the handles, but by 1938 these had been superseded.

Four
Cripplestyle and Crendell

The western parts of Alderholt are two separate hamlets. Cripplestyle and Crendall are on clays, with woodlands, and had many hurdle-makers and other woodland industries. In 1889 the Congregational History *described Cripplegate as 'scarcely three houses found together …. Upon their holdings the people built a cottage, and though they may have had to toil as hard as any day labourer, there was a feeling of independence. The house, often a poor one with mud walls, was their own in a sense [they were tenants] and so were the fields, which they, or their fathers, had enclosed from the surrounding wastes of heath and furze'. By 1899 many of these cob cottages were tumbling down. Crendell and Cripplestyle are still rural, not built up like so much of Verwood.*

Looking along Daggons Road, *c.* 1900, with King Barrow on the edge of the heathland in the distance. The pairs of cottages are brick, built in the later nineteenth century by farmers or landowners for their tenants, not the cob cottages which people built for themselves.

The Congregational chapel at Cripplestyle, just north of Verwood, built in 1807, and later extended a little. It was one of the simplest non-conformist chapels, built of cob and brick with a thatched roof. The Congregational history records the congregation building the chapel: 'After the day's ordinary toil was over, they set to, the men digging and working the clay, and the women gathering heath [heather] from the common to bind it together'. The clay and heather formed the cob walls. Even when extended it was only forty-five feet long, smaller than many cottages. The building was carefully preserved after a new chapel was built close by, but collapsed after the drought in 1976, and had to be demolished.

47 INTERIOR, CONGREGATIONAL CHAPEL. BUILT 1807.

Inside the Congregational chapel at Cripplestyle. It was usually called the Ebenezer chapel, after the Old Testament memorial stone thanking God for his help. Many non-conformist chapels took this name. The fittings inside were very plain, with two galleries (one visible on the right) to increase the number of sittings, and a pulpit with a little staircase. Congregationalists and Baptists were important in the Verwood area, despite the great inroads made by Methodism in the nineteenth century.

Two views of the chapel in 1974, only two years before it collapsed. Below can be seen one of the galleries.

The many members of the Sunday school at Cripplestyle, outside their new Sunday school building at the opening in 1907. Stephen Pope is towards the right.

Stephen Pope of Cripplestyle, who died in 1926, aged eighty. He was a fervent Congregationalist and superintendent of the Sunday school, a small farmer who 'lived a quiet life in the wooded wastes of north Dorset (*Dorset Year Book* 1931). He was particularly attached to the little old chapel at Cripplestyle, and was one of the church members who walked in procession from that old chapel to the new one in 1888: 'there were tears of regret in his eyes, not unmingled with joy. What that old thatched building meant to him no words can tell'.

The Congregationalists from Cripplestyle chapel have always held an annual Whit Thursday gathering when 'The school children, headed by a brass band, walked up to Kingsbarrow Hill, where a short service was held, and afterwards returned to tea: friends gathered from every direction, and in all sorts of conveyances; some years nearly a thousand were present to show their sympathy with the good pastor and help him in his work'. (*Congregational History*, 1899). The photograph above shows King Barrow. On Whit Thursday a flag was placed on the very top inscribed FEED MY LAMBS. King Barrow is 324 feet high, and on a clear day from the top the white cliffs of the Isle of Wight are visible, and, it is said, the very top of the spire of Salisbury Cathedral. The procession to King Barrow can be seen (below); the band are just visible.

After the procession to King Barrow, the congregation returned to the Old Chapel for tea, and the band played outside. Someone who took part in the 1930s as a child remembered the tea 'served in large pottery mugs glazed in different colours, in which was the strongest, hottest yet most welcome drink I remember. Boiling the water for tea was a task traditionally discharged by another family. Large billy cans were boiled over a fire in a niche cut out of a grassy bank. Meanwhile the band played suitable music surrounded by admirers who were too late for the

first sitting in the Old Chapel'. Children are seen here listening to the band outside the Old Chapel during Whit Thursday celebrations, 1930s. The EBENEZER painted over the door is clear. After the tea, the congregation marched to the new chapel for evening service. The Whit Thursday celebration continues at Cripplestyle, and the march still centres around the site of the old chapel.

The Sunday school outside the new Cripplestyle Congregational chapel before the First World War. The new chapel was built in 1888, and was named the Williams Memorial Chapel after the man who had been minister for forty years. The Old Chapel only had two ministers over the seventy years it was in use.

The Revd Whatley in the Williams Memorial Chapel in the 1920s. The fittings are much more elaborate than those in the Old Chapel.

A Crendell Methodist church outing in the 1930s. From left to right are: Mr Almer (driver), Joan Gray, Kate and Albert Rideout (Sunday school Superintendent), Ethel and Esther Gray, Reg Zebedee, Vera Lockyer, Arthur Zebedee (standing in doorway), Dora Zebedee.

The Deacons of the Cripplestyle Congregational chapel, with the minister (centre). The background has been whitened out, but a lorry wheel oddly appears between the two seated (right). From left to right, back row: Arthur Bailey, Alf Lockyer, John Sims, Wilfred Foster, Fred Sims. Front row: Frank Lockyer, Revd Walter West, John Bailey.

A neat pair of labourers' cottages between Cripplestyle and Crendell, known as Post Box Cottages. The style is typical of the 'improved' cottages built by big estates from the 1850s. The little Tudor mouldings over the door and windows are characteristic. The new model cottages were a huge improvement on the old thatched hovels, but belonged to the landowners, not the people who lived there. There is another identical pair close by: they were probably built in the 1870s, and the photograph is probably 1880s.

The Methodist chapel at Crendell, built in 1870 to replace a little cob chapel built around 1840. Part of the chapel was used as a Methodist day-school in the nineteenth century. The chapel is very isolated, with a little green outside and only one cottage close by.

Hay-making at the Zebedee farm, 1930s. From left to right are: Reg Zebedee (with a bandaged hand), Arthur George Zebedee (young boy), Arthur Zebedee, Harry Burbridge.

Reg Zebedee's favourite horse 'Bess' with a small hayrick built around a frame in the background. Much of the hay would have been eaten by her. Cliff Lockyer worked for the Zebedees in 1930s, and remembers the farm of approximately 100 acres, with two horses, fourteen or fifteen cows, calves, around 100 hens, a dozen ducks, a few geese and about twenty pigs. They grew potatoes, hay, corn, mangels and other roots. All the corn was still sown by hand, using a seedlip, a heart-shaped bucket which fitted closely to the body. Judging the amount of seed as well as spreading it evenly needed great skill, and when full, the seedlip weighed over half a hundredweight.

Reginald Zebedee with his bicycle, probably 1918-20.

Rita Zebedee looking tiny on one of the farm horses in 1941.

Reginald Zebedee with his
daughter Dora, *c.* 1934/5.

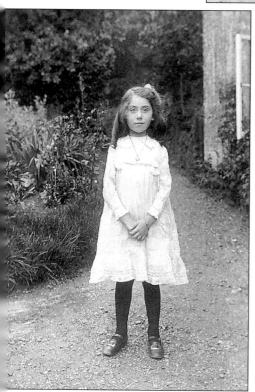

Mildred Fry, a cousin of the Zebedees,
c. 1910.

Hand-moulding bricks at the China Cottage Brickyard, Crendell, *c.* 1890. Harry Bailey is on the left. Machines had taken over this job in larger brickyards.

Harry Bailey's family Christmas card for 1906. Like many in the area, he was a small holder as well as working in the brickyard. His wife Annie (née Palmer) is holding the milking stool, and in front is their son Arthur William George Bailey. Their cottage still survives opposite the Williams Memorial Chapel.

To wish you the old, old wish,

A merry Christmas and a Happy New Year.

Five

Alderholt

Alderholt was a hamlet in the huge parish of Cranborne until it was separated in 1894. The parish spreads from the village (which is on clay and was very wooded) down across the heathlands to Verwood. In 1891 the population was 696, and it was only about 800 in 1975, when main drainage arrived and the area started to be developed. By the 1990s, the population was nearly 3,000.

Mrs Nicklen outside her cottage in Hillbury Road, Alderholt, probably around 1910-1920. The cottage survives, but it is no longer thatched. The bricks were probably made locally: the cottage dates from the early nineteenth century.

Two views of the main road through Alderholt, *c.* 1910. All the cottages and houses were recent when the photograph was taken, mostly dating from between 1880 and 1910.

Mrs Hayter outside The Terrace, Alderholt, *c.*1910. She looks the ideal mother and, perhaps suitably, is remembered in Alderholt as 'John Hayter's mother'.

The Post Office, Daggons Road, Alderholt. A rather more elaborate building than most, with a decorative band of terracotta around its middle. This may have been made locally.

Palmer's grocery, on the main road Alderholt, *c.* 1905. Children are lined up outside the shop, and a trap pulled by a donkey has stopped in the road.

The same shop a few years later, probably around 1910-14. From the left are Percy, George and Harry Palmer, brothers who ran the shop with their mother. Harry, the middle brother, was killed at Gallipoli in the First World War.

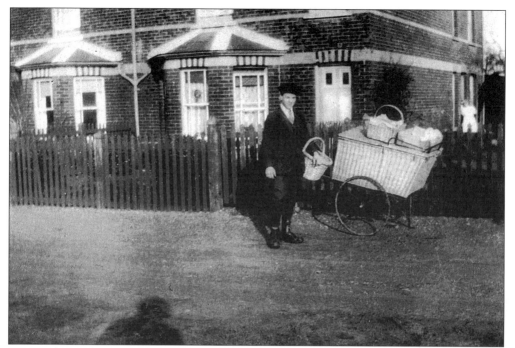

Percy Palmer, the youngest of the three brothers from the grocery, delivering bread with a handcart, outside Coronation Villas at Camel Green.

Thomas Pressey had opened another grocery in Alderholt by 1931, and he also owned a shop in Sandleheath (nearby but in Hampshire) by the later 1930s when this van was photographed.

Mrs Bailey outside her cottage at Alderholt. She is remembered as having the perfect garden. There were several Bailey families in Alderholt, and one hopes this is not the Emily Bailey whose gravestone also records the deaths of three of her daughters (one aged thirty-six, one aged twenty and one an infant) and four of her grandchildren. Emily herself died in 1938, aged seventy-eight.

The shop at Charing Cross, Alderholt, *c.* 1910. There is still a grocery here.

The school at Alderholt, in 1918. It was built in 1847, and much enlarged in 1874.

Mr G. Mann, head of the school (1874-1908), with the younger pupils in 1891.

St James church, Alderholt, is an unusual building with oddly stepped gables. It was built in 1849, and the opening was celebrated with a great rural fête with dancing and beer on the green which then survived beside the church.

A cottage, since demolished, near the church at Alderholt, c. 1910. Morning Glory plants have been trained around the door and window, and even reach to the first floor. Mr Nicklen (seated) looks several generations older than his daughter. He is plainly dressed, while she is very fashionable, with a pretty hat and leg-o-mutton sleeves to her blouse. Many rural girls went into service and returned home with 'towny' fashions.

Two fine gardens, probably belonging to the same family. Above are Mr and Mrs Rose, whose cottage was on the way to Manor Farm. Below is Mr Rose, with some wonderful runner beans. The two men have similar styles in clothes and hats: perhaps they are father and son. Both photographs date from around 1910.

Two views of Camel Green, south of the main road at Alderholt and now built over. Most of the houses in these photographs from between 1900 and 1910 are late-nineteenth century. The 1898 Directory lists three brick-makers in Alderholt: they must have been kept busy supplying bricks for all the new local buildings.

The Churchill Arms, Daggons Road, Alderholt changes very little between these two photographs (above: 1950s, below: *c.* 1900). Only the cart shed (with trap, below) has been filled in to make a shed or store.

Alderholt Park was built in around 1810, away to the north of the village. The rather plain original house can be seen in the background (above) with what looks like the whole of Alderholt posed in front, probably in the 1880s. Whatever was being celebrated needed a band: it may have been a Friendly Society annual feast, or a Sunday school treat. Below is Alderholt Park as rebuilt in the later nineteenth century, with exotic plants on the terrace. The postcard dates from around 1906.

One of the lodges (East Lodge) to Alderholt Park, *c.* 1905. It still survives. The Churchill family lived at Alderholt Park from 1854 until the 1920s. Muddlingly, another large house in the parish was called Alderholt Lodge, easy to mistake for the real lodges to Alderholt Park. In the mid-nineteenth century, Alderholt abutted Wiltshire as well as Hampshire, and the first Churchill owner of Alderholt Park boasted that he had flushed a duck in Dorset, shot it in Hampshire and picked it up in Wiltshire.

Alderholt Road shows more typical houses for the area. Fred Hibbard, carpenter and parish clerk lived in the left-hand house from the 1920s, and made coffins in the shed in the middle.

Two methods of delivering milk at Alderholt, around 1900-1910. Above, photograph shows a pony and trap carrying the churn. Left, the churn is balanced on a wheeled attachment to a bicycle. In both cases the milk would have been measured into customer's own jugs: bottles were still in the future. Fred Bailey (with the bicycle) also had a greengrocery, and grew some of the produce in his own glasshouses.

Mr Woodvine (left) and his son, *c.* 1910, possibly simply gardening, or possibly starting to sink a well. Behind is the Independent chapel which was demolished in the 1950s. It stood opposite the Congregational chapel.

Sunday school outing, *c.* 1900, believed to be from the Independent chapel, Alderholt. There is a good load for one horse. The wagon was one normally used on the farm.

The Station, Alderholt, *c.* 1907. Mrs Brewer, Alderholt Postmistress, can be seen on the platform, along with Bill Bartlett. When the station opened in January 1876, it was called Alderholt, but five months later the name was changed to Daggons Road because there had been confusion with Aldershot. The line was closed in 1964.

Repairing the bridge which took the railway across the road to Alderholt Mill in around 1900. There are many workmen here, and lots of cows.

807 BRICKWORKS, ALDERHOLT

The Hants, Wilts and Dorset Brick Company had big premises near Daggon's Road station, served by their own railway siding. The two big chimneys seen here were built by 1901. There had been brick-making on a smaller scale in Alderholt for centuries.

The workers at the brickworks by the station, probably 1930s.

The laying of the dedication stones at the new Congregational chapel, Alderholt, July 1923. There were fourteen of the stones, seen standing clear of the start of the walls in both photographs. The payment for the stones (£2) helped towards the cost of building, and a brick cost £1. Some stones were memorials, but most of them were from members of the congregation. The Pastor and the Sunday school each paid for one, as did the Band of Hope.

OPENING NEW CHAPEL ALDERHOLT JULY 16

The crowd at the opening ceremony of the chapel, later in the same year as the laying of the dedication stones, 1923.

The completed chapel: the porch has been altered, and a parish hall added next door, but otherwise it is still the same. The 1920s were an unusual time for chapel building; most of them date from the later nineteenth century. Alderholt had been planning a new chapel from early in the century, but the First World War delayed it. The site had been dedicated for some time before building started, which is why there were already graves there when the foundations were laid.

The Alderholt Congregational Sunday school in procession with their banner, probably late 1920s. The minister is Mr Baines.

Edith Pinhorne (neé Ford) at the age of eighteen. She was born in Alderholt and went into service in Onslow Gardens, London, returning to Alderholt to marry. She was born in 1892, died in 1986 and is buried at the Congregational chapel, Alderholt. Doubtless she took part as a child in processions like the one above (top of page). One of the dedication stones at the chapel is to A. and R. Pinhorne, her parents-in-law.

Alderholt Mill from the bridge, *c.* 1906. All the buildings survive, and make a picturesque scene. There are many more trees today. Dorset, Wiltshire and Hampshire used to join by the mill, and there was an old local saying that a man standing in the stream in one county, could touch two more counties with his hands.

Two Brownies at Alderholt in the 1930s, with Mrs Duffett and her son Ron. The Guides were founded in 1910 (the Scouts in 1907) and an organisation for younger girls soon followed, known at first as the Rosebuds. They became the Brownies in 1915, named not after their brown uniform but after a traditional benevolent fairy. A great boost was given to the movement by Princess Mary becoming President in 1920. She visited Dorset in May 1930 for a huge Dorset Guides rally at Kingston Maurward near Dorchester.

These three evocative postcards (including opposite top) show Alderholt's Coronation celebrations, 8 July 1911. The coronation of George V was actually on 29 June, but a few places, like Alderholt, decided to hold their events a week later. They were very wise: it poured with rain on the 29th and was fine on the 8th. Above: a very well-decorated wagon with Britannia holding a Union Jack shield, oddly led by a clown. Bottom: some inhabitants are in fancy dress, but most of the girls are in best white dresses with fancy hats. Triumphal arches were a vital part of later-nineteenth and early-twentieth century celebrations, and this is a particularly artistic example.

The mounted police should have been leading the procession, but as was usual at that date, the cyclists got there first.

Alderholt children in fancy dress, quite probably for the same 1911 coronation celebrations. The wagon looks just the same as the one Britannia is in.

Steam-threshing set at Alderholt, around 1890-1900. Charlie Pinhorne is the man with a pitchfork (centre). The steam traction engine probably dates from the 1880s: the men on the skyline are standing on the huge threshing machine worked from the fly-wheel of the traction engine via the belt. The corn was taken from the rick (like the one on the left) and fed into the thresher which 'threshed' the corn from the straw and fed the corn into sacks. Cliff Lockyer remembers the hurdle-makers and timber cutters coming to help on his father's farm at Gold Oak, Alderholt, when the threshing machine visited. His mother would lay out food and drink in the barn. Six to eight people, besides the driver and his helper who came with the set, were needed to feed the machine and make the straw stack. As a boy, Cliff loved to see the whole set of threshing tackle on the move – engine, elevator, straw tier and the sleeping van. Coming round corners, they filled the whole road, and often the verge too.

Cutting a field of wheat at Alderholt, c. 1930. The crop is tall, and the straw may have been intended for thatching. It is being cut with an old self-binder, probably originally horse-drawn. The tractor (a Fordson) probably dates from the 1920s, and has iron wheels with cleats.

Six
Wimborne St Giles

The ancient parish of Wimborne St Giles extends down to the heathlands at Verwood, but most of it is on clay and then the chalklands. The village is small, but has the mansion of the Shaftesburys and an old church. In 1906 Frederick Treves described it: 'The village, composed mainly of modern red-brick cottages, is severely prim and tidy, and parades the air of being much pampered and well-endowed'. A great contrast to Verwood – no pampering there.

A thatched brick cottage at Wimborne St Giles, c. 1910. Although the village is so close to Verwood it is very different. The eighteenth-century cottages at Wimborne St Giles, even humble ones like this example, were built from brick rather than the cob used at Verwood.

The 7th Lord Shaftesbury (right) outside his house at Wimborne St Giles in the 1860s, one of the earliest photographs in the whole area. This Lord Shaftesbury was the great reformer and philanthropist, and inherited the estate in 1851. He was horrified by the condition of the agricultural labourers and by their squalid cottages. He set to work building new 'model'

cottages and improving conditions generally, but he was hampered by his land agent who was dishonest and swindled his employer of large sums of money. The big house dates from the seventeenth and eighteenth centuries, but the big tower was added in 1853 for the 7th Earl.

The 9th Earl of Shaftesbury with King George (sixth from left, standing) and Queen Mary (third from left, seated) at Wimborne St Giles, probably soon after George's accession to the throne in 1910. Shaftesbury had been Chamberlain to Queen Mary when she was Princess of Wales. The north window in the rebuilt church of St Giles is dedicated to the coronation of George V. The 9th Earl came into his inheritance, when he was only seventeen, in 1886 and lived until 1961. When the Prince and Princess of Wales visited Wimborne St Giles for the first time in October 1908 they arrived at Verwood by special train. The platform 'had been specially decorated with flowers and an arch was erected over the station gates'. The school children were waiting outside the station and lustily cheered the Royal party as they motored away'.

The gardens at Wimborne St Giles, around 1910-15, just the time King George visited. There were formal terraces around the house, and a huge old avenue of trees.

St Giles Lodge, Wimborne St Giles, a very decorative little building, *c.* 1900. It was called East Lodge, and was built for Mr and Mrs Perry. Mr Perry was one of Lord Shaftesbury's gardeners. Mrs Girgan, the Perrys' daughter, now aged 104, remembers Lady Shaftesbury watching the building of the Lodge.

Cold frames and gardeners' bothy in the gardens at Wimborne St Giles, around 1900-1910. Three of the gardeners are taking the cover off one of the large cold frames.

The Cutler family (inside the garden) at Wimborne St Giles, *c.* 1900, with four unknown visitors at their gate. Rosanna and Kate are by the gate, then Bert, Horace, Martin and Frank, all of whom were carpenters on the St Giles estate, except Martin (with the beard) who was a builder, undertaker and blacksmith. Also listed in the Directory for 1907 is Joseph Cutler 'sheep trough maker (wood)'.

Fanny Fry standing by the stocks at Wimborne St Giles, 1930s. The stocks have a little roof over them to protect the ancient remains of an old form of punishment; they still survive.

Men of the Dorset and Hants Yeomanry in camp at Wimborne St Giles, May 1914. Lord Shaftesbury was in command of the South-western Mounted Brigade, which included the Dorset, Hants, Wilts and Somerset Yeomanry, and numbered 1,000 men and officers almost all with their own horses. The Hants and Dorset soldiers were camping on his estate. The Yeomanry were mobilized immediately on the outbreak of war, only two months after this camp, and were posted to Norfolk. By 1915 they were at Gallipoli, where seven out of eight officers and 60% of other ranks were killed or injured in one single advance. The Yeomanry were part-time soldiers, and their main training was at annual camps like this one, which was the last before the First World War.

The Wimborne St Giles Home Guard during the Second World War. The fifty men all lived locally, and as with all Home Guards, did their normal work as well as army duties. Many were farmers or farm labourers (reserved occupations who were not called up into the full-time army) and others worked for Lord Shaftesbury. In the front row, fourth from the right, is Lord Shaftesbury, who served as an ordinary soldier in the Home Guard, despite having been a Brigadier-General during the First World War. As Lord Lieutenant of Dorset, he carried out an official inspection of his own unit of the Home Guard, and also took the salute at a march past of the Home Guard which included his platoon. Mr James Carter (fifth from right, front row), was in charge of the Wimborne St Giles platoon, and was head gamekeeper on the estate. From left to right, back row: George Bedford (farmer's son), Roy Pinhorne t.d., -?-, Bill Brewer, -?- (gamekeeper for Lord Shaftesbury), Walt Wrixon t.d., George Scott, Henry Wharton (gamekeeper for Lord Shaftesbury), -?-, Ron Pinhorne t.d., Ron 'Reemer' Doe t.d., -?-, -?-, -?-. Second row: Ken Riman (gardener to the parson), Jack Renyard f.w., Sidney Fry (shepherd), Joe Selby f.w., Tom Pitman f.w., Stan Doe f.w., Blondie Selby f.w., ? Way (farmer), Chubby Butler (farmer), Bob Snow (farmer's son), Reg Renyard (carter), -?-. Third row: George Hankins (gardener), Smiler Wilson (chauffeur to Lord Shaftesbury), -?-, Ernie Clark (estate timber cutter), Charlie Flippance (gardener), Dick Shepherd (tenant farmer's son), Bob Perry, Bert Pinhorne (worker at watercress beds), Bert Butler (coalman), Charlie Doe f.w., Ivor 'Ducky' Dowding (gardener), Ernie Green f.w. Front row: Len Parkes f.w., ? Williams (estate worker), -?-, Art Pinhorne (road worker), Bill Churchill t.d., Darkie Henning (smallholder), Sarge Curry (chauffeur to Lord Ashley), J. Carter (Head Gamekeeper), -?-, Lord Shaftesbury, Albert Steel (carter), Bill Fry (farmer), Duncan Wallis t.d. (key: t.d. means tractor driver; f.w. farm worker.)

95

Inside the church at Wimborne St Giles on 1 October 1908. The eighteenth-century church caught fire on 30 September: the roof and most of the fittings were destroyed. Workmen had been soldering in the tower, and it seems likely that they caused the fire, which was first noticed at midnight by some labourers who were walking by. The fire engine was swiftly brought from the big house close by, and a man on a bicycle set off to fetch the Wimborne Fire Brigade. The Wimborne firemen were overtaken on their way to the fire by Lord Shaftesbury's motor car occupied by his agent who picked up the Captain, two men and a quantity of hose and rushed them to St Giles, but they were too late; even the church bells had melted. The two views shown are looking east (above) and west (below). The huge roof beams lie on the floor, but the stone pillars are remarkably unscathed. They later had to be demolished and replaced.

The almshouses next to the church were lucky to survive. The church looks very odd with no roof. Scaffolding (above) was soon erected to stop the tower falling. The church had been restored and altered in the 1880s.

The masons working on the restoration of St Giles church. All that was saved from the old church was the pulpit, a few seats, the font and the altar rail. Six new circular pillars were built to support the ceiling (two can be seen in the photograph). The new ceiling was of 'fibrous plaster'. The church re-opened only two years after the fire, and was lit by the very modern electricity, supplied from the big house. The organ was powered in the same way.

A new peal of six bells was cast for the restored church, and the tower was strengthened to take them. Three of the bells were memorials: this one, the treble, was given by Mrs Ashton (who took this photograph of it) in memory of her husband Mr Henry Ashton. It is inscribed *Veni Sancte Spiritus Adeste Fideles* and dedicated to the Holy Spirit. The Wimborne St Giles bell-ringers rang the first peal on the new bells before the opening service of the rebuilt church, and the ringers from St Peter's Bournemouth rang another peal immediately afterwards.

Edwin Fry, gamekeeper to the Wimborne St Giles Estate. He is seen here at Brockingham Beeches (left) probably 1950s, and with gun and dog.

Sidney and Fanny Fry outside their cottage at Wimborne St Giles in the 1930s. Sidney was shepherd to a farmer in Wimborne St Giles called Mr Shepherd, which must have caused muddles. Their cottage has since been demolished.

Sheep-shearing at South Monkton Farm, Wimborne St Giles in 1941. Sheep were the basis of all farming on the chalk, and hand shearing was a long hard job. Here it is taking place inside a large barn, with hurdles used as dividers (and to hang coats on). The sheep are penned behind the hurdles. By the 1940s virtually every farm was using mechanical clippers which speeded the job up, but here it was still being done by hand. The big sack is probably hanging open to receive the fleeces.

Seven

Horton

Horton is an old village and parish, with a great variety of geology. The western third of the parish is chalk; the middle clays and the eastern third is heathland running down to Verwood at Horton Common. In 1901 Horton only had 331 inhabitants: it had been much larger in area before the new parish of Woodlands was carved out of it in the 1870s.

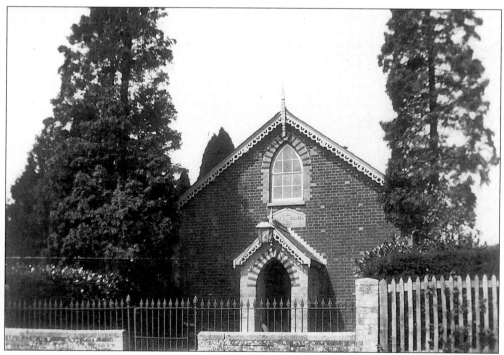

The little Methodist chapel on Horton Heath, probably in the early 1930s. The chapel was built in 1877, and still looks exactly the same, even down to the trees surrounding it. All around the land is still heath. There has been a Methodist congregation at Horton Heath since the late eighteenth century.

The church of St Wolfrida at Horton was founded in the tenth century, and was part of a nunnery. Wolfrida was an early abbess here. The photograph (above) of the chancel, probably around 1900, is unusual as there are very few showing a church service in progress. The reredos behind the altar has been painted recently, but otherwise the scene looks much the same. An external view of the church (below): St Wolfridas seems eighteenth century externally because the walls were refaced in brick then, and the windows rebuilt. The little spire is very unusual and dates from the 1720s. The church is L-shaped. The postcard probably dates from around 1910.

Preparing an extension of the graveyard at Horton, probably in the 1930s. It is very odd to see ploughing so near a church. Lord Shaftesbury had given an old orchard for the extension.

More land preparation at Horton church. Clearing the graveyard (above) in the later 1940s, using four-prong forks to remove couch grass. Walter Still and Chubby Chandler (left with forks) and Allis Chalmers smiling on the right (he must have been nick-named after the tractors). The flat-bed trailer is the descendant of the four-wheel wagon seen in earlier photographs. Below are Ken Wharton (left) and his father Henry Wharton. The elaborate centre in the tractor wheel is a set of strakes, which could be pulled out to enclose the tyre. The strakes then gave more grip, but they needed to be retractable as they could not be used on the road.

A celebration in Horton, *c.* 1910. It looks a little subdued to be the Coronation celebrations of 1911, and is probably the school fête held in early August each year. In 1910, *The East Dorset Herald* reported that, after being marched to church for a service 'the children proceeded to a field near the church, where plenty of amusement was provided in the way of shooting galleries, swing boats, stalls etc., and tea'. Dancing to the strains of the local band was enjoyed by the adults later in the evening.

Horton Cricket Team in 1935. From left to right, back row: Mr Bowditch, Mr Isaacs (umpire), Bob Loader, Albert Steele, Jack Selby, Arnold Hayter, Mr Bracher (umpire). Front row: Sam Thorne (his horse and van was used to transport the team), Fred Isaacs, Jimmy Steele, Chris Frampton, Walt Potter, Ernie Isaacs, Albert Sweatland.

The Primitive Methodist chapel at Haythorn Common in around 1901. The thatched cottage behind is unusually long. Haythorne chapel was rebuilt in 1888, the time when many of the early-nineteenth century cob chapels in the area were replaced by larger brick ones. At Holtwood nearby, all the bricks for the new chapel of 1904 were given by members of the congregation who were brick-makers.

HORTON.

A general view of Horton, around 1900-1910, showing the village centre with its few thatched cottages. The land is all farmed, in contrast to the heathlands just to the east.

The whole village seems to have come out to watch the hunt at Horton around 1900-1910. The two women cyclists have the best chance of keeping up with the horses. Clump Hill is on the edge of the heathland between Horton and Three Legged Cross, at Horton Heath. The pines were probably part of early-nineteenth century attempts at heathland reclamation.

The opening of the village pump, Horton, 1901. The pump and its handsome shelter were given to the village by W.H.J. Carter, and survives in good condition. The bill shows that the whole structure cost £55 14s, including the roof.

The children of Horton school in 1910. The population of the parish was only 405 at the 1911 census, and the average attendance at the school was forty-six, so these forty-five children with two teachers represent the normal total. The children range in age a good deal – those at the front only look about four, and some of the larger ones seem into their teens. In 1911 the village of Horton had five farmers, three of them on the Heath and probably with only a small amount

of land. In the village itself was one inn, a post office, a draper, a grocer and one policeman. Surprisingly there was another shop on the Heath, and a woman cow-keeper who would have looked after grazing cows for their owners. The rest of the parents of these children would have been agricultural labourers, or small-holders or brick makers, thought too insignificant to be listed in the *Directory*.

The Old Pond on the outskirts of Horton, c. 1906. Horton had a pottery industry in the seventeenth and early-eighteenth century, and there was probably brick production too. The potters and brick-makers were unpopular for leaving hazardous ponds behind after they had dug the clay. This pond was probably an old clay pit.

An American Allis Chalmers crawler tractor at work in Horton in the 1950s, driven by Ken Wharton. Crawlers, despite the advantage of spreading their weight on the land, have always been less common than conventionally-wheeled tractors. Dorset War Agricultural Committee registered this tractor along with two other identical ones in June 1946.

Another American tractor at Horton – a Case, again driven by Ken Wharton.

Working in the fields at Horton in the 1950s. An unusually realistic photograph showing Ken Wharton driving a Minneapolis Moline (made in America) and Charlie Chandler standing beside it.

The Horton Inn, away to the west of the village on one of the main through roads, *c.* 1906.

The simple late-eighteenth century staircase at the Horton Inn had a wooden gate at the bottom to keep dogs (and children) off the stairs. These gates were quite common in larger houses and inns, and are very practical.

An early car outside the Horton Inn, around 1906-10. The car seems to be a Darracq, probably a 20hp model of 1906/07. These French cars were popular in Dorset – in 1905 five were registered out of a total of seventy-one cars, and in 1907 another four out of a total of ninety-seven. The boy holds what is almost certainly a locally-made besom broom: he and the man on the left must have been working in the stables, soon to be made redundant by the motor-car. Like so many roadside inns, Horton Inn had been important when it was a coaching stop, but after the railways took over it was pretty well deserted. The building dates from the late-eighteenth century, the peak of coaching and the time when many inns were rebuilt. Cycling brought some trade back to roadside inns in the later-nineteenth century, but it was the motorcar which really set them up again.

Charles Harper visited the Horton Inn, around 1903, finding it 'a fine, substantial old house, once depending upon a great coaching and posting traffic, and even now that only an occasional cyclist stays the night, dispensing good-old-fashioned, solid comforts'. (*The Hardy Country* 1904).

In the 1930s the landlord was Bob Loder, who was keen on the history of Wessex, and preserved the ancient courtroom at the inn where the manorial courts had met. He had decorated it with signed portraits of local landowners. Also preserved was the old brewery at the back, complete with its vats and coppers (*Dorset County Chronicle*, 19 September 1935). When it was sold in 1949 the Horton Inn had 'six excellent bedrooms' and four more in the attic, but only one bathroom.

A group from Horton at the British Empire Exhibition, Wembley. It seems a long way to travel in a char-a-banc. The simplicity of the womens' clothes (and the shortness of their skirts) is a huge contrast with the slightly earlier photograph below. The British Empire Exhibition was a sensation when it opened in 1924, with its super-modern plain buildings of concrete. The huge displays included all the countries of the Empire, and Palaces of Industry, Engineering and Arts. Seventeen and a half million people visited the Exhibition in 1924, and it was re-opened in 1925 to allow even more to see it. Front row right: Reg and Gladys Thorne; woman with case Olive Seeviour and left of her Alfy Dear; then Mr Seeviour. Back right Bill Blake, and the two women together are Dorothy and Dolly Seeviour.

Horton people at a local fête, c. 1910. The banner behind the fourth man from the left reads 'Horton', and possibly they are visiting a fête like the large one held most years at nearby Wimborne St Giles. Horton seems not to have had a fête at this time, only a children's day which was unlikely to have had big marquees like that here.

Eight
Holt

Holt extends from heathlands to clay, with the small main village on the clay. It only became a separate parish in 1894: until then it was part of the huge parish of Wimborne. Unusually for Dorset there is a large village green and almost everything in Holt is on or near that green. From at least the eleventh century, the area which is now Holt parish was a forest, owned by the King, where hunting deer (and keeping rabbits) was more important than agriculture. It remained in royal hands until the seventeenth century.

All the children of Holt seem to have posed here for the photographer on the green at Holt, around 1900-1910. The school was close by. All the cottages are thatched, but unlike Verwood, they are of brick, or brick and timber framing.

The Post Office, Holt, around 1900-1910. The brick cottage probably dates from the eighteenth century, and typically has a curvy roof-line to accommodate the windows of the upper storey. With cob the line is usually straight to give more strength. Hamlets around Holt have more thatched cottages and wonderful names like God's Blessing Green, Pig Oak, Broom Hill, Crooked Withies, and Summerlug Hill.

The Old Inn next to the church at Holt, around 1900-1910. In fact, the building is not old, and must have been largely rebuilt in 1898 as a datestone records. Like most village pubs, cycling improved its trade from the 1880s: several bikes are parked outside.

The village school at Holt, with all the pupils outside. It was next to the green. The school was founded in the 1840s, and by 1847 there were fifty-eight boys and sixty girls being educated there. It was a church school, and in the later nineteenth century the vicar visited the school almost daily. It cost a penny a week per child, but was largely supported by local subscriptions.

The Revd Cecil George Paget became vicar of Holt in 1884, and this Christmas card probably dates from that year. He has drawn a tiny version of Horton tower (left) and a sketchy church. The ill-proportioned horse looks bored. Revd Paget was treasurer and correspondent to the school at Holt.

Bowers Farm, Holt, *c*. 1930. All through the 1930s the farmer was George Brine. The farmhouse is mid-eighteenth century, built from brick. There is now a huge neo-Georgian house, but many of the barns survive. In the 1930s farming was still much as it had been in Victorian times. Horses were the main motive power, and many men were needed to work the land. Bowers Farm was a typical mixed farm, growing crops and keeping animals. Almost certainly, the cows

were still being milked by hand, and huge amounts of labour were needed to make the hay and harvest the corn, and yet more to get both into the ricks. The corn would remain in the ricks until it was threshed to separate grain and straw: the hay would be fed to the beasts from the rick.

The farmyard at Bowers Farm was large, and lined out with old farm buildings. Top: a couple of the cows in the yard, with their winter quarters behind – the single-storey barn with slatted wooden walls. The gaps top and bottom were for ventilation. Bottom: Posing with the bull outside the taller barn. He is held on a bull-pull, a stick attached to the ring in his nose, and on a sort of halter as well. Behind the bull is a 'parked' hurdle: they were still common in the 1930s.

The card shed at Bowers, 1930s, with a two-wheeled dung put parked inside. The children are in a more elegant vehicle – a two-wheeled trap.

Pigs in the yard – a fine saddle-back with her little ones. The barn behind clearly shows several stages of construction – vertical and horizontal boarding, brick bases to the walls and unusual sliding doors.

In the fields at Bowers Farm, 1930s. Above: gathering up hay. The picture has been posed: the hay rake (left) would have been working ahead of the wagon to collect up the hay, which was then loaded on the wagon by hand using the pitchforks. Below: cutting corn, probably oats, with a self-binder pulled by two horses. The crop seems rather light. The oats, like the hay, would have been needed to feed the horses and cattle on the farm.

Making a hayrick at Bowers Farm in the 1930s. Unloading the wagon with the rick behind. The hay is probably clover, often grown for animal fodder. Behind is a rick which has already been thatched with straw to keep the rain out.

A very strange photograph, thought to be milkmaids at a barn in Holt, c. 1930. There are at least fourteen of them, far too many to be working on one farm, and they are dressed up to the nines with cross-over aprons, full length, and very fancy caps. Some have white protective sleeves over the lower part of their arms, and generally they look like dairymaids who produced cheese and butter. The barn could be the one at Bowers, before the doors were altered, and the women could be nurses rather than dairy maids: a complete puzzle and a fascinating picture.

The milking herd at Bowers returning to the fields, 1930s. They are short horns, the usual dairy cow of the period.

The farm dog sitting on the wall sunning himself in another part of the farmyard

Nine

Three Legged Cross

Three Legged Cross (or Three Cross, as it is often called) in the southern part of Verwood has been known by that name since the sixteenth century, referring to the three-way road junction. The hamlet was described in 1899 as 'somewhat bleak … although many parts are now cultivated, there are still extensive heaths'. In the 1830s the Congregationalists resolved to try to establish a chapel there, because there was no place of worship, 'but the movement was at first very unpopular among them, interfering as it did with their usual way of spending the Sabbath in drinking and fighting' (Congregational History, 1899)

Birch Tree Farm, Three Legged Cross, c. 1910. The couple by the porch are probably Mr and Mrs Harry Orman. The cottage is built of cob, and the lines between each stage of building are clear. Many more cob cottages survive in Three Cross than Verwood itself, and this is a large one. Some are so tiny that it is difficult to believe that they can fit two storeys in.

Inside the corrugated iron church at Three Legged Cross, probably around 1910. It was built in 1893 as a mission church. Chapels were much more important in Three Cross, like the rest of the area: there were both Congregational and Methodist ones. The Congregational chapels had a stable for the congregation's horses because the population was so dispersed that people had to travel long distances for services

The centre of Three Legged Cross, *c.* 1910. Three traps and bicycle then, but today busy traffic. Besides the Traveller's Rest pub (right) there was also a Post Office, a grocer and a blacksmith in 1911.

Harry Stevens Shepherd Orman (1850-1932) was one of the fourteen broom-makers listed at Three Cross in 1908, so the besom-broom visible behind him is very appropriate. He seems to be standing outside the porch of Birch Tree Farm (see p. 125).

The two girls are probably Harry Orman's daughters at Birch Tree Farm with the family pony who is harnessed with a collar for a trap or wagon, not for riding. Harry Orman probably farmed a smallholding as well as making brooms. The name of the farm reflects the many birches of the area which were used for broom-making.

Three Legged Cross in the 1930s, a typical heathland scene with only a few brick cottages and smallholdings.

West Moors Common, *c.* 1910, a reminder that the heathlands continued to meet the sea at Bournemouth. Verwood and area form the north-eastern corner of the county, and the top of the northward tongue of heathland, but the heaths originally extended south-east in the New Forest, south-west to Dorchester as well as south to Bournemouth. Apart from the New Forest, much has been reclaimed for agriculture or simply built over.